THE DEPLORABLES V.

THE DESPICABLES:

"DEFENDING THE RIGHT TO BE HEARD!"

By

Dennis Andrew Ball,

author, THE BALL DOCTRINE:

"Creating Peace & Prosperity In Every Nation!"

ISBN 13: 9781076284457
10: 1076284450

DEDICATION

"THIS BOOK IS DEDICATED TO AMERICANS

WHO SACRIFICE EVERYDAY TO PRESERVE

PROTECT & DEFEND OUR LIBERTY AND

FREEDOM FOR OUR CHILDREN AND

GENERATIONS TO COME! NOW THE TIME

HAS COME FOR A NEW GENERATION OF

AMERICANS TO TAKE THE REIGNS OF

STATE & MAKE THEM WORK AS THEIR OWN

IN THE BEST INTERSTS OF THE PEOPLE,

THEIR CHILDREN, THEIR FAMILIES AND

GENERATIONS TO COME!"

TABLE OF CONTENTS

Dedication

Acknowledgment

Authors' Foreword

———

ACKNOWLEDGMENT

To The COURAGE Of President John Adams Demonstrated At A Time Of Great Promise To Our Nation During The Early Times Of American History.

Author's Foreword

I am reminded by history past the history of the United States would not be complete if it were not for those gallant men and women who in the face of danger, proceeded to do something Special about it! America's very existence is tied to her economic health which has seen a great deal of danger for THE PEOPLE since 1913 starting at Jekyl Island, Georgia by a group of elitist Domestic & International bankers with the participation of the Congress of the United States on Christmas Eve. We are living in time where our nation is divided by forces adverse to the sustainability Of the American traditional family and our children.

5

Since the death of President Kennedy, events in America and the World have continued to show all of us how vulnerable our society has become by governments adverse to the best interests of the American People & their families, particularly their Children &n Seniors and the Congress of these United States, the result being a bloated deficit with borrowing and spending unaccountable to The Citizenry & States of the United States; including fiscal policies, laws and acts contrary to The BEST INTERESTS of ALL Americans.

As a result, American Society has changed adverse to our laws, attitudes & culture that created stability within society, the traditional family.

Now, that is being assaulted by government officials and social attitudes that are unhealthy and divisive resulting in a mental health crisis of massive proportions supported by real statistics.

Now is the time to explore the cause & effect Relationship of our culture demonstrating adversely to its history and heritage. It is a serious Problem eating at the heart of the nation. We must come clean with each other and support the Transformation for our children & generations to come.

1. A NATION AT ODDS.

The *history of America* would not be complete if it were not for the men and women who sacrificed so much of themselves for a new nation and its children. Of course, much can be said of those who plotted against them and used them to profit at their expense. For those they must answer for us we must correct their mistakes for our children and generations to come. This then, becomes the back ground and back drop of *defending the Right to be Heard!*

"You cannot help the poor by destroying the Rich." "You cannot keep out of trouble by spending more than you earn." "You cannot lift the wage earner by pulling down the wage payer" – Abraham Lincoln

---

"I have always been afraid of banks."

"One man with courage makes a majority"

"It is to be regretted that the rich and powerful too often bend the acts of government to their own selfish purposes." "Take time to deliberate but when the time for action arrives, stop thinking and go in." – *Andrew Jackson*

Let it be said, that America's finest hours are yet to come because the Children Of America can make a contribution to not only our Nation but also the World!

We are the product of generations past, present and future with the belief that our rights come from God; NOT THE STATE at a great cost to those who fought and died for them! That was the Social Contract created in 1781 at Yorktown-Gloucester Bay, Virginia.

The monuments laid at the reefs of those so honored are a testament to the sacrifice of so many for the hope that their sacrifice would *bear.* A proud nation was born and with it the greatest nation on earth in the history of man, "*AMERICA!*"

9

THE NATIONAL BACKGROUND

Early History

What was assumed by those in power was taken for granted by those struggling to live out their dreams. *AMERICA* was a land of opportunity because it's people made it their priority to continue living out their dreams for a better life for themselves and those for their children.

Colonial America grew at an astounding rate by the span of time from the founding of the Republic at Jamestown, Virginia 1607 until the last entry known as Georgia Colony 1732.

Of course, many events in between the time of founding and establishing Colonial life dominated the culture legally and politically; particularly making it possible for 2.5 million people to realize their value because the Bible was read in the home, the schools and the Supreme Court! Ethics & Morales were also taught in the home practicing honesty and

10

good business including honest services. The attitudes within the culture was fairness as the colonies grew in population and farming. As a result, the *Great Migration* ensued so that by the beginning of the War For Independence, *AMERICA* had enough population to fight England for it. And so we did on July 4, 1776 by way of the Declaration Of Independence, Congress, Philadelphia, Pennsylvania.

Now comes DEFENDING THE RIGHTY TO BE HEARD. What does it say and what does it mean?

From KEEPING AMERICA STRONG AGAIN, I have attempted to prove and provide the winning strategy to strengthen the American economic system to conform with Constitutional guarantees of *due process* ignored by every President since Kennedy!

But in a more transparent way, Defending The Right To Be Heard means addressing both the abuses and solutions in relationships

11

that cause concern relevant to culture and attitudes, two of the most caustic problems of our age.

Unlike generations past where the institution was sacred & supported, today's society places it as a trophy to be paraded then discarded by the players.

In a mere 75 years attitudes changed that now risk a total and complete Social Collapse toward attitudes that threaten even the most committed.

The *forgotten family* has been discarded made to *suffer* by the callous and evil behavior of our Institutions and its leaders including Judges, Lawyers, Politicians, Legislators, Business leaders, Trade Unions and a *Shadow Government Unaccountable to no one!* The Rule Of Law has been ignored and with it the forgotten society!

THE DEPLORABLES are those who the left consider undesirable with contempt the sheep

of Bernie Sanders & Hillary Clinton who
coined the term, a "Basket 0f Deplorables."

2. THE NEED FOR CLARITY.

Since the early 70's, America has continued to experience a downward cycle ever since the death of President Kennedy.

Vietnam, Arab Oil Embargo, Unions, Foreign competition all made their dent including the disaster called WATERGATE.

Government spending continued to rise even with the election of a fiscal conservative in Ronald Reagan. Debt continued to pile up while the Gross National Product declined creating a trade deficit in the $Billions$ of dollars.

This in turn gave rise to the dot com bubble with the signing of the "Free Trade" agreement known as NAFTA. Since then, every President since Bill Clinton has failed to correct a spiraling federal deficit impacting the quality of life upon the American family.

Since 9/11 American industry has lost

14

over 50,000 factories and counting. It is a wasteland in areas that were buzzing with COMMERCE and manufacturing products. Some communities are engaged in making Unions accountable to their members to protect them from job loss in the event the worker's factory relocates.

But as late as May, 2011 this author was proposing to reverse this trend away from America to bring capital back to our shores by means to support the families of the United States Of America.

Which raises the question, "How Would You Do It?" Besides creating a tide that lifts all boats, the cost of production and materials compared elsewhere, becomes the economic engine that drives supporting the middle class family.

If we learn anything from the last three Presidents, it is that the means of production is vital in order to create an economic engine!

Factories just don't happen! They require an educated work base in skills necessary to do the job.

Management is responsible for creating a work environment that is both conducive to worker productivity and compensation. One without the other is insufficient and causes lack of worker productivity and apathy which leads to termination.

Failure on the part of any party engaged in this process, spells certain disaster that has come to visit our shores. Reversing this trend makes it imperative that business, labor and government get on the same page to correct the abuses in the system impacting the labor force.

Raising a family on minimum wage is impossible needing the support of a living wage requiring a restructuring of the economic system to create the incentives for "Making America Strong!"

16

Undoubtedly, that responsibility lays with the community and how they wish to approach the problem. However, ultimately The task of educating and financing job creation will require creating a work base that makes our nation productive.

Socialism be damned! Free-enterprise Capitalism on a level playing field will erase a gross trade imbalance and bring American jobs back to our shores.

Capital to do that will come from industry that has parked its profits off shore waiting to reinvest in America and her people! Trade deals that place American jobs at risk will be no more. The American worker and their family must become "Number #1" for our nation and her children.

In "KEEPING AMERICA STRONG AGAIN", I discuss what must happen to create a new economic system for America to recover from years of abuse since 1913.

The clarity of knowing the differences between living wage jobs and minimum wage is immense and requires us to investigate what is driving the divide or division in our country.

Can it be we have entered into a new age that attacks the good from the bad? Are we useful idiots in the cosmos to be overthrown by despots?

Is our future at risk because we fail to question why we are being divided as a Society by power and greed coming from government officials both elected and unelected?

Has OUR social institutions failed us making us vulnerable to being destroyed and our heritage with it? Can we stop the tide of cynicism that assaults our values & harms our children?

Choose ye today whom you will serve!

3. BLOCKING THE DIVIDE.

"The moral of the story is that for people to be safe they must be protected from personal exploitation by any entity so inclined."

Our homes are only as safe as the economic health and wellbeing of our economic system. Most Citizens are devoid of this knowledge as are politicians who simply do not care as long as their own interests are served.

President Kennedy also spoke by his words and deeds both prior and after his death for he had put into motion policies that are still alive today recognized to keep the family safe.

The question most important that must be Answered by all of us to the extent we work for the Best Interests of our family, then who's interests are we working?.

To abuse others and make our nation weak is a crime against humanity. "Free Speech" is a right to express facts and opinions We The People are granted by The Constitution. It is not a license to destroy one's life or character.

The divide intensified during the radical 60's due to the activities of anti-American groups protesting the Vietnam War causing it to harm the families and the values we cherish.

Watergate was a product of this condition that affirmed the distrust and dislike of one group against another.

Our national heritage has been on trial ever since. I am reminded it is We The People who are to govern this great country but only if we take it seriously to act and do what must be done.

Local, State and Federal government is the responsibility of WE THE PEOPLE. Look to yourselves when things fail you. Not your neighbor. They maybe as ignorant as you are to the realities surrounding them and their family.

That is why you must invest your time in

learning what is important in life making yourselves strong in the knowledge of "family" and what is necessary to maintain and sustain it. This is a community effort to bring industry back to the United States to employ our people and secure our nation.

THE DESPICABLES hate this because they are bankrupt morally, ethically, emotionally. There lives are empty filled with hate for God, hate for others, family & themselves. Lovers of self more than lovers of God they plot and plan the destruction of anyone who calls them out to stop them. A gang mentality takes over justifying themselves.

OUT OF CONTROL, their despicable behavior shows how sick they truly are wishing to cause injury to innocent people who are as Vulnerable to their acts of crime against all of us.

Their goal to shut us down only provokes more determination in us to see that either they walk away from their life style or be crushed by it. There is no alternative to this narrative.

The universal principles that determine human events within the economy of life are exacting and predictable. This is not theology but real life economy proven by years of historical documentation.

When you think you have it all over others, the Universal principles of life kick in and will kick you to the curb if not kill you.

In my mothers' adult guardianship case, over ten different individuals have died since her death in April, 2006.

The Bible speaks of this in Galatians 5:6-7. "God is not mocked and whatsoever a person Soes, that they surely shall reap."

Those who come against us have made themselves victims of their device. See how this works. Life is a constant but governed by it's own rules. Every tyrant is eliminated in the time span they ruled. It is true for a country, a nation, a continent, and a World.

The Universal laws of nature that the Creator put in motion rule this planet. Negligence and abuse are always met with a knockout punch coming from somewhere at sometime by somebody. Don't believe it? Try it! For we live and move and have our being in him who loves us and gave his life for us. Who is this person. The Unknown God? Acts 17:28.

4. A DISEASE WITHIN.

Not enough is said about the abuse our culture has created upon its people. Our social mentality is blighted by the sheer numbers required to survive in an ever ending spiral of social and economic decline.

. *For* profit corporations have replaced those who once looked to families to care for the sick and the elderly. Prison overcrowding too! All with a mandate by governments both State and Federal that suck us dry and makes us weak. Enough!

Families Are Forever and must be affirmed in and by any society. Why? Because there is only one race, the human race and emulates the values that support the worth of children and their role in society.

Because they are our greatest asset, we must *not* abuse them but alternatively help them succeed where Society has failed.

That failure resides within both the economic and social institutions that have ground to a halt because of the negligent behavior coming from Washington D.C. and State Governors who have a duty to uphold the virtues of the traditional heterosexual nuclear family to make and keep it strong within their own community.

How can they do it you ask? Several ways. Principally by making their first priority restoring the economic health and vitality within their own locality.

How can Illinois be responsible for what does or does not happen in Missouri or Iowa? The movers & shakers in those communities may have some interest in mineral and water rights, but cannot be expected to change the economic and social climate of others until & unless they are able to address concerns that are their own.

To go along to get along those days are

gone. We The People are faced with an economic and social crisis that mirrors in some areas during the great depression; especially within certain minorities and ethnicity groups.

"Every Man A King" in his own right makes for good publicity by people like Huey Long, former governor of Louisiana. Problem is it does not address the opposite need to work in the Family's Best Interest as a Social model for *Real Change!*

That comes when the local community decides to get to work to improving the quality of life for all; not just some! I will speak further about that in *NO CHILD LEFT BEHIND!*

Can we do better? You bet we can! Our public resolve for our children is a testament of how committed we are to doing that which must be done! Our families too! How can we work in their

26

Best Interests and deny them the support they need to survive and thrive. That would be sacrilege upon the most vulnerable members of society.

Our hearts go out to families destroyed by neglect, indifference or sheer violence that destroys their ability to function & survive. Our culture has grown weary of those who prey upon it for their own profit by any means harming the very members that make it work. This is unacceptable and must be Stopped!

Violence begins in the heart so the good book extolls. "Vengeance" is mine thus sayeth the Lord! For all that it's worth, I too have trouble but dedicate myself to the virtues and ideals upon which economic and social justice rest at "HOME". There is where we get our values and our commitments to guide our lives in the direction they will go.

My prayer is for everyone reading these

27

will come to the same conclusion I have that Families Are Forever and should be treated as such in a community of caring and educated people for their children and generations to come.

Once we do the commitment, then we are on our way to bringing the change we all desire, need and require for our children and generations to come. We must educate our kids to know right from wrong and motivate them to be the best they can be. We parents, have a great responsibility to raise up a child in the path they should go and at the end they will not depart from what they were taught.

We must become educated ourselves to know the ways and wiles of the World and those close to us. The reading of my texts is a good start along with focus groups to talk about the BEST INTERESTS of the family and what that *really* means!

As before, our hearts go out to those

touched by tragedy in today's society. Everyday, we read about *death* at the door of Citizens' being victimized by others from opposite ends of the social economic ladder.

I am reminded how difficult it is to correct events others create for us that bring harm into our lives. But I pray that you will find it within yourself to do that which must get done to resolve for yourself the damage that was done or being done to you and your loved ones right now! FAMILIES ARE FOREVER AND THEY REQUIRE OUR SUPPORT TO SURVIVE & THRIVE!

The path to prosperity is learning what must get done to do it. That's educating oneself learning skills and knowing how to learn. My prayer is that our efforts be focused on the institutions of learning including those within government made accountable.

5.TEACH CHILDREN WELL!

Learning is essential to the tasks of overcoming the racial divide in America. The World also must learn the path to racial and economic prosperity for her children & generations to come.

SOPHISTRY has literally changed the Mission & Purpose of Federal government to one of consumption & waste of Taxpayer dollars.

Entitlements, Earmarks, Pork, Mandates, Gerrymandering and getting re-elected with few term limits have caused a burgeoning national debt and crisis of confidence in our nation's economy and economic system.

How much more can the nation endure until real change addresses the real problems of Income Inequality? Only time will tell, but in this author's humble opinion, it needs to start NOW!

Our children will thank us for making it and them our priority to secure their futures and those to come.

Replacing the 16th Amendment with a Balance Budget Amendment makes sense. Bridling the Federal Budget from politicians who use their position to buy votes with tax payer dollars in the form of Pork, Earmarks Mandates, Entitlements, Sophistry is wrong!

How many school lunch programs for little kids are we depriving by masking our true intentions in ways that hurt our nation and our Children?

On the streets of Washington D.C. I witnessed in 2012 homeless people and families sleeping on the streets and sides of buildings for not enough food to eat or a place to sleep. In a country as rich as these United States, I saw what poverty does to people and the aftermath of hopelessness.

Skilled Labor prevents that social experience of homelessness. Making life affordable is the challenge we face and it starts with the budget economy that works for all Americans and their families. From there, Citizenship becomes the responsibility of us all to see our children are educated and our community productive. Skilled labor solves a multitude of problems politicians create.

A Balanced Budget amendment will keep Federal departments from overspending and gaming the system for more resources the next fiscal year. With the States processing the tax on consumption, they will be in the position to take control of the purse to empower them to control the size and depth of the Federal government because controls on spending and borrowing do not exist. It is within their discretion based on revenues collected at the State level to fund having the effect of limiting the size of government and its wasteful spending practices on non-essential services & programs based on the taxes in their control.

But to a larger degree, the idea that the vast majority of Americans pay NO Income Tax is a testament that something is wrong with this picture that must be corrected not only for the good of society but for the good Of the Country.

Teaching our children well teaches them

respect for themselves and introduces them to a culture that values them and opinions they have regardless of how little or how big they express them.

There in lays an opportunity for mothers and fathers to show their children the value and importance of communication in their relationships at an early age in development.

I am reminded as a child in my own childhood how ignorant I was to life's important reality's and lessons about our human development and its aftermath. How mothers communicate with daughters and fathers with their sons about attitudes that drive us and make us who we become!

It is tragic that despite the number of marriages each year the rate of divorce continues to be high amongst couples.

This shows a problem exists within the culture especially compared before and after World War II.

I attribute much of it to ignorance amongst the sexes especially during puberty and adolescence. Society's expectations are so low regarding interpersonal relationships that it becomes a contributing factor in keeping divorce lawyers busy in family courts.

Human beings as complex as they are tend to gravitate toward others they agree. However, within the area of interpersonal relationships between the sexes, intimacy is a major factor that often defines and drives them. This, I believe is a major contributing factor in the breakdown and failure in Western Society.

Until society is ready and willing to talk openly about human sexuality amongst the sexes, divorce will remain a constant to keep divorce lawyers & family courts in business.

'If you are not working in the Best Interests Of your family, who's interests are you working fore?'

Divorce after marriage is a mistake event that should be avoided by not marrying someone who does not share your values or motivations. Communicate with others your interests and desires within an interpersonal relationship so you know what is good or bad for you personally.

Don't assume anything but communicate so you can learn and know the likes and dislikes of others that make you feel good to be with them or not with them. If we wish to see our families restored, we will have to consider doing and communicating for our benefit. If failure persists, it means that the relationship has changed requiring action to cure for the other members. However, the tragedy is that it might have been avoided if more was known prior to the marriage and subsequent children it produced.

Our kids deserve better than what society in America is producing. Let us learn and grow together to solve family abuse amongst members by becoming educated in the area of interpersonal intimacy and its power to nourish or destroy intimate relationships.

Hold government accountable FOR acts criminal to the well being of THE PEOPLE!

6. THE DESPICABLES!

"The States Have The Responsibility For Administering, Collecting & Allocating The Sales Tax To The Treasury." – The Fair Tax

Because NO provision was written into The United States Constitution regulating Borrowing or spending by the Congress of these United States, there exists and has for years, a problem regulating the National Debt beginning in 1913 continuing until now.

That problem is DEFICIT SPENDING. borrowing and paying Interest on the Debt with taxpayer dollars out of the Federal Treasury. This is what George Washington warned America at its founding and to keep America "Free" from its burden as if foreign Army's had absconded with government

38

property without ever firing a shot!

In our history, the problem has grown to become UNACCOUNTABLE DEFICIT BORROWING & SPENDING making it IMPOSSIBLE for the Federal Government to police itself without shutting it down.;

Our history also shows that since 1913, *America* has failed to put in place safeguards to prevent this unaccountable cycle to come to an END!. WE THE PEOPLE, demand that this government stop it's endless cycle for the good of our Country, our Children and Generations to come!

The Ruling Banking Families in the Federal Reserve Central Bank know exactly the burden they have created by design upon the American people & their children. They know the bigger the debt on the nation the

greater their profits from the DEFICIT.
They are not about to reduce it because
they know they don't have too. But that
does not release them from the liability
of their FRAUD on the nation. Specifically,
Executive Order E.O 11110 signed June 4,
1963 by then President John Fitzgerald
Kennedy transferring control of America's
monetary system to the United States
Treasury.

We can see that in June 1963, America
Borrowed $305,859,632,996.41 backed by
Gold & Silver.   Today, the debt has grown
and keeps growing to unacceptable limits
all to make the Bankers more money on
interest charged on THEIR DEBT.

-Here's The Evidence-

From 1963 to 1999 The National debt climbed from $305,000,000,000.00 billions to over $5,000,000,000,000.00 trillions.in a matter of 36 years. Now it is approaching $20,000,000,000,000,.00 with trillions in Unfunded mandates stuck to the States.

The Cartel has made its business to loan the Federal Government any amount of *fiat* currency it requires as long as it pays the interest on the debt. They have also made it their business to cause harm to Citizens by causing the government to collect taxes to pay them. The debt however, cannot be paid *but it can be forgiven.*

How? Because it is backed by nothing! The same people who formed the Cartel sold the Country that the Banks would take care

41

of the financial needs of the nation so long as the nation paid them interest on the debt. The Federal Reserve System is neither Federal nor a Reserve of Currency nor a System. It is in effect a Banker's Cartel who lends *fiat currency with no value for interest payments to the members of the Cartel every month administered by the IRS & Treasury.*

This relationship was designed by the Scientists of the Federal Reserve System. They knew exactly what they should do to make the "System" work for them opposite the American Taxpayer.

In effect, it is a corrupt institution that Funds the International Monetary Fund & The World Bank.

There is absolutely no evidence that Executive Order 11110 signed June 4, 1963 has been rescinded or the wording that nullified it despite other President's issues.

We are left that since every President since Lyndon Johnson, has ignored it that perhaps fearful that if they were to follow its directive, they too might be killed. Both Lincoln and Kennedy believed the *Nation* should issue and regulate its own currency; not a foreign bank masquerading around as a Federal entity but a private banking cartel.

The nation had seen this before during the presidency of Andrew Jackson (1829-1837).

THE BANK OF THE UNITED STATES was shut down by Jackson but an attempt was made on his life. Jackson, founder of the Democratic Party surmised as warned by George Washington that the currency of the nation was sovereign to the United States Treasury and should stay in its control both in the manufacturing and minting of printed and coined currency.

The inflation non-backed currency wars on the dollar devaluing the dollars' worth in terms of purchasing power and payment of debt release. Diluting the economy with unbacked green backs is a recipe for more inflation and higher prices.

Backed securities with Gold or Silver makes for a much more stable economy disallowing the government from over spending and causing families harm by a reckless and selfish policy of greed.

Our children are at risk to the Federal government to economically fail because they will become 'slaves to the state" no longer able to control a rogue policy of self enrichment at the expense of the taxpayers and their families. The Federal government will have to learn to live within its means like Citizens must live within a budget. The Charter Bank will replace the Central Bank aka Federal Reserve System.

The boom and bust cycles in the *history* of the nation is over. Economic prosperity for America will be measured in real dollars backed by Gold or Silver instead of nothing!

The national debt will be gone and the dawning of a new era in funding will begin! War bonds, Saving Bonds, Treasury Bills all have their place raising money for worthy Causes and Investments for the The People!

The IRS, 16th Amendment, Federal Reserve Act, Income Tax should all go away

Leading to the introduction of a Fair Tax on Consumption or spending. Because half of America pays income tax, it is not fair to tax Income on those who do pay. A Fair Tax will mandate that everybody pays tax on what they spend. That is fair & equitable.

No income tax means individuals and families can keep more of their hard earned money for themselves to support their lives and their property, It also means they that control the purse controls the size of the government Local, State and Federal..

The Fair Tax does that at the point of sale incorporating a tax on goods & services equitably distributed for the benefit of the taxpayers. The effect is that reduced revenues means smaller government for our benefit and our families. This stops the

46

burgeoning tax burden and creates a system fair to WE THE PEOPLE!

Now industry can return to America because tax on income has been removed opening the market to financial prosperity for all.

Industry will find its way back building the factories employing the people creating economic prosperity and accountability for our children and generations to come. In effect, "NO CHILD LEFT BEHIND!"

THE DESPICABLES are those among us who use us to profit at our expense. Those in the employment of government services be they in the three branches have made it their business as accomplices in the War that defies reason taking advantage of WE THE PEOPLE in the Courts, State & Federal.

7. DESPICABLES AMONG US!

America's destiny demands her people do for her children that which requires their economic, emotional security, benefit and welfare for now and generations to come.

To do that means being educated in the misconduct of this government creating a new model by which its Citizens function.

Unlike the Federal Reserve System, A Fair Tax does not require an Amendment to the Constitution to make it work. It is suggested and recommended for a Balance Budget Amendment replace it to keep the government's budget in check with its income.

Since 1913, the Federal government is dependent on tax and spend policies that cause harm to our children and families.

Inflation on prices of goods and services can be directly attributed to the number of non-backed currency dollars floating from the Federal Reserve Bank. Whether its an entry on their computers, the debt continues to grow which the cartel wants to realize the income on interest that debt generates to it.

Why this is allowed to continue should be of great concern to The People of the United States. Until this is changed and a new model appears, *America* will continue to be held hostage to the bankers and their *cartel* families.

In addition, the *National Debt* as a Product of the Gross National Product (GDP) is comprised of Public, Foreign Countries, and Americans. But the Federal Reserve Banks lend to the Federal government and that debt should go away. That would reduce the National Debt by 70% with the reset owed to trusts and countries.

That would greatly reduce the stress created on the taxpayers to support the debt. In effect it would relieve the burden on the people to keep more of their hard earned dollars in their pockets thereby increasing their ability to save and build an equity for themselves and their families.

DESPICABLES AMONG US:
PROBATE ABUSE IN STATE COURTS!

Now, that all said, my greatest concern is that your money and property will go away from you and your family by those in the Judiciary of State Probate Courts.

In my first book "AMERICA 2000:

"Foundations For Generations! I speak of the economic abuse done to innocent family members by State Sponsored Guardianship proceedings that abscond with ALL OUR MONEY & PROPERTY.

These proceedings are conducted by Probate Courts on the County level with the State Bar, Supreme Court & Legislature participating. It amounts to a whole sale scam of that person's property and assets into the pockets of third parties who had nothing to do to earn it or interest in protecting it. In other words, Probate Courts are nothing less than agents of SWINDLE upon the families of America.

Some have compared them to Courts of Human Trafficking & a new form of slavery they once were used during that period in

American history. Human ownership by Proxy by State Governments has returned to our shores by a hell bent Judiciary to suck every penny out of the family and make sure it is accomplished before they die!

The practice is so wide spread, families plundered, pilfered and thrust into poverty within a short period of time from the initial proceedings. It is a threat to every American who has accumulated any assets & property over their lifetime.

These tyrannical proceedings are destroying the Republic as it was not intended allowing criminal elements to profit at the expense of THE PEOPLE!

It is also occurring in the Family Courts. Children held for ransom being kidnapped and placed in another system of corruption where money from Title IV-E funding has destroyed the sanctity of the home and made children chattel to be controlled and used for State profit. This was instituted during the Clinton administration by Hillary & Bill Clinton, setting a very bad precedent for our nation & future for our Children & families.

Title IV-E Social Security Act:

As if Probate Courts weren't enough to cause us harm, the Clinton's made sure that children and their parents would be a Bonanza for State governments to profit & destroy.

Title IV-E of the Social Security Act is lengthy as it is cumbersome by design. Law-makers purposely create titles and sections to cause confusion in the administration of the Act. It is designed to reward those

53

making decisions for parents and children who have not their Best Interests and are only doing it for money paid them at the State level by the Federal government entitlement programs. They are Despicables!

The Clintons' knew the damage this would do the nation's children by separating them from their parents. It also allowed Big-Pharma ample opportunity to profit manufacturing neuro-inhibitors to mess with their brains at a young age. This is criminal making it probable that the laws must be repealed and amended out of the language.

My concern is that children have a good Childhood free from the shenanigans of the State Courts using laws that do harm to families and their children.

Society requires strong families to

survive and thrive; not the watered down dilution the State has to dish out by making money off them!

This is the way of the World, its legal system, attorneys, courts and judges. Hillary Clinton is an attorney; so was Bill Clinton. Both of them did tremendous harm to the family unit that is currently in repair by the likes of those individuals who identify the problems and are engaged in doing and changing the outcome.

The Young & The Old are targeted as Profit centers for the State. This must Change. Our Society has gone secular in its attitudes toward parents and children and justify their intentions in the "Best Interests of the Child." Yet children go without and suffer at the hands of adults removed from

55

their lives and not part of their parents lives.

This is not in the Family's Best Interests!

THESE ARE THE DESPICABLES!

JUDGES who use their bench to profit at the expense of families. Who find no fault in and of themselves transferring ownership of one's personal property into the hands of 3rd parties who had no economic interest until they were handed it by the Courts.

Even & including the transfer of custody of minor children into the care of strangers for the sole purpose of making money.

56

8. OUR RIGHT TO BE HEARD!

As though time and distance could be seen into a looking glass what is to come, history shows us what has happened to nations when the laws of economic$ are violated by those in authority.

No doubt, the nations of the World still have much to learn from the mistakes of previous generations culminating in their demise. The graph below illustrates nations' who in fact make those mistakes.

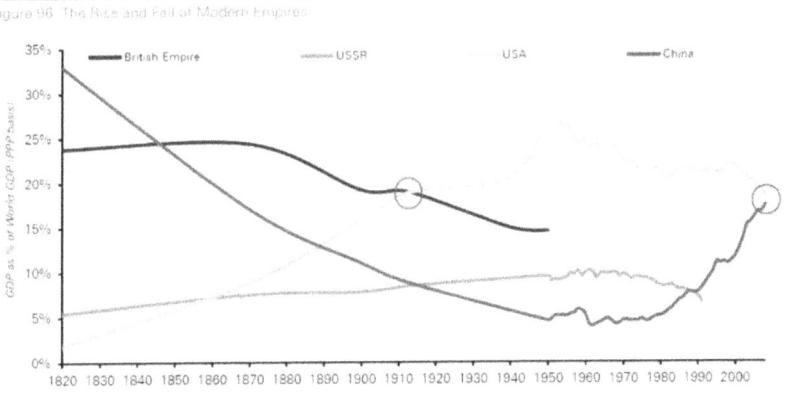

It would appear to this author that for years the economic policies that created mass chaos within market conditions are based on the notion that profits trump the BEST INTERESTS of people, particularly those with the ability to exploit others for personal gain. These are the Despicables.

THE BALL DOCTRINE points out the absolute need to *reign-in* the money powers that have created so much harm to so many people throughout World History. This was President Kennedy's vision:

'He believed the family *reigned supreme* as the basic social unit of every nation'.

Speech after speech, the affirmations of America's global supremacy over those nation's who created harm to the national security of the United States and its foreign policy directives were met head on by the Kennedy administration. Kennedy was a man of *destiny* and his policies created serious challenges for the establishment.

To that end, I have attempted to show what is lacking in the economic health of the nation. Central banks cause harm in the modern world because their policies are corrupted from within by policies created in 1910 and beyond starting at *Jekyl Island, Georgia. These are also the Despicables!*

What is needed now is an act that corrects and cancels the harm that began over 100 years ago.

'THE BALL ACT' makes it possible. Conceived in *Liberty*, the act affirms the treason of Woodrow Wilson signing the

Federal Reserve Act on December 23, 1913 while Congress was out of session during Christmas.

A progressive, he violated his Oath of Office as President allowing enemies of The People to exploit the Constitution! As long as Central Banks could charge the federal government interest on non-backed money, the corrupt establishment allowed it to pass. President Kennedy knew the Constitutional Powers of Separation of the three branches of government and that in effect it was the United States Treasury should be in control of America's *monetary and currency policy.*

This violation of America's sovereignty showed Kennedy what previous Presidents also knew: 'The issuing of money was to come through Congress; not a Central Bank!

In other words, the nation's business was to stay with the nation; affirmed by previous generations and their administrations. Third party Central Banks is what Andrew Jackson shut down The Bank Of The United States during his presidency in 1833 & paid off the national debt with funds from the federal treasury backed by gold and silver bullion.

The founders had warned the nation that monetary policy could be circumvented; the nation threatened by policy violating the sovereignty of the United States causing the loss of all that had been fought and died.

With the signing of Executive Order 11110, President Kennedy effectively shut down the Federal Reserve System and they were alarmed; especially the families who benefit & support it. America's sovereignty was reaffirmed and the national debt was in check. The nation was on its way to policies that would lead to greatness amongst the World's nations affirming free-enterprise Capitalism superior to Marxist-Socialist Communism in the struggle of ideas for World dominance.

The result of this act will be to return American sovereignty back to itself with a new tax system eliminating the need for its Citizens to pay interest on debt. A balance budget insures the government stays within its means to pay for what it spends. Gold & Silver returns to back government issued Tender regulated by the States as to moneys Collected from the Fair Tax on spending.

Other debt to Trust funds & Foreign Countries paid back to refund our debt.

9. STAYING STRONG!

With the advent that *positive* change makes on the nation and the world, The People will be vilified. Years of abuse by an intrusive and corrupt system of swindle and scandal will finally be gone never to return.

The Federal Reserve System has its Tentacles in the International Monetary Fund (IMF) and the World Bank (WB).

Every nation is vulnerable to the Central Bank policy of *fiat capital* like Problems it creates in Greece & Venezuela.

The Bankers have created a fail proof System of banking that works for them at expense of their depositors. By weakening the dollar through dumping dollars into the market, prices rise because it takes more of it to pay for essential goods and services in relationship to the nation's Gross National Product (GNP). President Kennedy was all over it and knew that it could bankrupt the country; something he wanted to prevent!

I believe Robert Kennedy had he become President would have continued the policies his older brother created.

Both Kennedy brothers knew that War & Money corrupt a country. Both were against the exploitation of both. That is what the bankers wanted tied to The Federal Reserve System. From it, it can be conjectured that David Rockefeller and his Tri-lateral Commission & Council of Foreign Relations have directly benefited from the power the bankers have created by this debt creating system of *fiat capital*.

10. MOVING AHEAD.

What I have attempted to explain & show is that our political and economic system is under attack by powers adverse to the *family* of the United States and to a larger extent the entire World.

Despicables in the Political, Economic & Judicial cosmos have done great harm to all of us considered a *Basket of Deplorables.* It must STOP!

> *"If your not working for your family, whom are you working fore?"*

An important question everyone must answer. My hope is that exposing forces opposed to Law will force a change that makes a necessary correction for society that will cause our children to thank us. Their *futures* are our responsibility NOW!